SHADOWS THAT STAY

STRONGEST OF HUMANS, AT TWILIGHT, BECOME FOOLS IN LOVE.

MOHITA

Made with ♥ on the Notion Press Platform
www.notionpress.com

"To mom and dad,

Who lovingly supported my book addiction and never questioned my madness of reading. Thanks for all the research material."

Contents

Foreword	*vii*
Preface	*ix*
Acknowledgements	*xi*
Prologue	*xiii*
1. He[art]	1
2. Childhood	2
3. Regrets I Wish Stayed.	4
4. Bloodlines	5
5. An Autum Ode	7
6. Pretending To Be A Mask	9
7. False Hope	11
8. The Graveyards- I Found Myself There.	12
9. Never Same	13
10. Canvases	14
11. Isn't Love A War Of Humanity Too?	15
12. Palates That Bleed	16
13. A Lost Entry	17
14. A Lost Entry-II	18
15. A Lost Entry-III	19
16. Love And Crosses	20
17. Loudness Silenced	21
18. Orchids.	22
19. Gift Wrapped Scars	24
20. Westerlies.	25
21. Religion.	26
22. We.	27

Contents

23. Letting Go. 28

24. Bougainvillea. 30

25. Rose Colored Window Panes. 31

26. A Known Stranger. 32

27. Drunk And In Love. 33

28. Goodbyes. 34

29. She. 36

30. Hushed Truth. 38

31. The Other Person. 40

32. Cityscapes, Darkness And Mistakes. 42

33. Chasing Skies-looking For You. 43

34. Firsts. 45

35. I Ramble Words As Dusk Sets. 46

36. Happily Ever After. 48

37. To, 49

38. Falling. 51

39. Meet Me Soon. 52

40. Warnings. 54

41. A Wanted Death. 55

42. Home. 56

43. Ancient Maps. 57

44. One Last Time. 58

Connect With the Author. 59

Foreword

Tapestry of man's nature is to know the unknown and sometimes in the journey lose themselves. This book captures moments of profound insight.

As you turn the pages may you find peace, inspiration and a connection with the language of poetry. The lines invite you to pause, reflect and embrace the power of words.

I hope these words somewhere will be the voice of your thoughts too.

Preface

Within these pages, you will find the echoes of laughter and tears, the whispers of love and longing, and the vibrant colors of our shared existence. Poetry, like a key, unlocks the doors to the chambers of our souls, allowing us to explore the profound and the mundane, the beautiful and the raw.

As you traverse this poetic terrain, I hope you discover pieces of yourself mirrored in the verses and that you are transported to realms you've never before imagined. Let these poems be your companions on a voyage of reflection, introspection, and inspiration.

Welcome to this collection of verses; may they resonate with your heart and stir your soul.

Mohita.

Acknowledgements

I'd like to express my deepest gratitude to all those who have supported and inspired me in my poetic journey. Your encouragement and belief in my words have made this book possible.

To all my muses,

Who are the backbone of these writings(both good and bad).

And lastly,

To my caffeine for the countless late night companionship.

Thanks for keeping me awake.

Prologue

A sonnet to all the emotions and muses I've met, they aren't prevalent anymore but they definitely stay within me and all the times I've written about them,

They've told me memories make great manuscripts.

1. He[art]

I don't ask him to read me my favorite stories anymore. Afraid he'd call me selfish for wanting my love back.
A year ago on 4th of October, I told him amidst a conversation " I'm pretty bad at loving everything that has a heart, [and you- wanting you would be the death of me] "
When he held my hand that dreary afternoon- the ghosts of my past cried -
For no one had ever touched them with such pure pain-
And for no pain had ever felt so sweet- so much that the macabre lines of my palm,
started believing destinies existed.
I don't tell him I want him to be my forever anymore- afraid I'd betray my fate of being alone
[people have often told me I'm better off when the world doesn't see my wounds]
The mirror in my car says " objects are closer than they appear "
[I wish it was talking about you]
He always used to love me the most after telling me I'm awful-
But don't people always speak the truth in anger?
I still don't know if I should wait-
For neither did he believe in forever nor did he say goodbye,
~M

2. Childhood

There's a dusty attic in the room I called ' Childhood '
It reeked of glass and blood and paint and wood
It hauls me to itself ; more often than not.
Calling me to ask about some answers that I owe to it.
Sometimes in the afternoon when the sun enlivens the scars around my ribs
I pack some doughnuts, a latte and go there willingly.
We sit there on the burning hickory.
As the tainted concrete stares at us ; hollow-eyed yet full of tales.
We reminisce the stories that hang on each color.
And the regret and shame that we have hidden over the years,
Under the layers of paint.
Rain,pelts on the rose colored window,
We laughed at our wounds and struggle as we try to love the people that trapped us there.
People we cared about , people who weren't strangers ,
People we knew.
I promise to get it the answers- the next time I visited,
That pisses it off.
After all its a little impatient, a little furious, a little dangerous and a lot like me.
It's my worst enemy.
Completing the jigsaws of each other- like quintessence of love-
We fill up each other's void.
For some mistakes we committed; some scars that never left.

Maybe they will live until the cosmic end.
Even after we are long gone.

3. Regrets i wish stayed.

Would love feel a lot more like regret-
If I ever walked into the quiet waves because living had become too much baggage-
If I ever painted your name on my books- on my favorite happy endings-
Bruises of your love look like portraits on my heart
Would my hands be qualified enough to hold yours?
Would you like me more if I said less??
Would love feel a little less like regret?
If you and I never met.

4. Bloodlines

How angry you must have been at the reflection that created you
thrusting you into war at such a tender age-
They pity me as I walk on the streets-
Sometimes I stop by to tell them -
" I'm what shame silence suppression and pain created
I'm a museum of wounds-
I take scrapes of leftover love as dinner-
But her blood that runs in my veins- Starves Me.
I tell them I am a Visage of all the wrong kinds of love-
My mother was hatred filled with rage."
I see my dad's love through the bruises she painted on my heart-
My sister's concern feels like thorns all because it touches the stitches around my veins-
Every fall when her demons turn her heart into a block of nothingness
She takes away some of my warmth to protect herself
Lovingly and almost delicately she stitches back the wounds-
Every October I get a little colder
She tells me as an elder daughter-
born into the legacy of void love-
I'm bound to take up the alll the winters my ancestors passed down.
I sit as she braids my hair
The flowers she puts are a homage to all her vain attempts to touch my heart [how do you even reach a place thats almost non existent]
I love the infinite multiverse theory because it means somewhere my bloodline wasn't a testament of pain.

In a parallel universe my grandmother told me a story about a solider she saw back in her days -
And not the battles in her mind
Where my mother is not hungry for love[she believes the only good parts of her were passed down to me]
And where home doesnt mean a place I attempt to escape.

5. An autum ode

Where are you today?
How are you?
At an intrepid hour-
Inside the words of my book
I found you in my sleepy thoughts-
People say eternal peace is soothing-
They don't know what it's like to taste a nuance of you-
I remember how you had waltzed across the room with my hand in yours
You kept looking at the floor-
Hoping the words that were carbon printed on your trachea somehow loosen up-
And yet you were afraid when they make their way out of your mind and into my ears-
You'd just end up wanting her back.
The Choreography of cosmic symphony-
You twirl me and catch me in a few milliseconds-
5 milliseconds to be precise-
All that time wishing maybe I'd change into her-
Last October you had whispered into our embrace " I wish I have you forever "
Whilst- engraving her name in your veins
How poetic of you to hold me with bloodied hands-
Even if the blood belongs to someone else.
I watched us fall in love

You watched us fall apart.
Maybe some infinities are bigger than others
At an ungodly hour.
I see the bougainvillea singing of heartbreak-
I see our stars colliding and separating.
And I write you a letter asking a number of questions
Most importantly-
Where are you today?
How are you?

6. Pretending to be a mask

It was my flaw of hiding behind a life made of pearl and quartz,
My imperfections being excuses to hurt the ones I love.
There was this guy I met,
Told him my poetry was damned,
That I believed there was a price for every smile.
He filled my void with the universe,
Said " All of it is flawed,
That's how you know you're a part of it.
That's how you know you're alive. "
There were some drowning waves,
I held on to some hyacinth for life.
They saved me from themseleves,
Said " The world shouldn't have to pay for our depth and shallowness "

There was a tainted trauma,
The flames of a past in holocaust
Everything I held dear destroyed to ash.
Told the ones I cared about to leave,
They left.
Assured myself I can't expect the whole world to pay for my unhappy childhood.
I walked as a post-war city, an unfathomable loss,
Searching for a new continent, Losing myself in the seas as I travelled,
He held my hand and pulled me back,
A world of blurred tones and lavender potraits,

And whispered " Stay, darling. Love doesn't always have to be sad. "

7. False Hope

Being alive and in love is a tragic business.
I look at your smile and know that you can do better.
A black hole of sorrows engulf me tonight,
You hold a comforting lantern on the shore,
A soothing balm to my gaping wounds.
I am too afraid to tell you for I know it won't last,
Too afraid to give you hope, when I know I'll take it away,
Your dark black eyes, swallow me
As you gaze at me across the table,
I am too afraid to look back,
For I know they won't let me walk away.

8. The Graveyards- I found myself there.

Burying everything that we were, before that morning last summer- when we met.
We become a little dead, a little heartless and a little colder tonight.
Digging deep into the ground as we let go of all the love,
And filling the grave, we toss our words for dirt and pour out the last of our tears
Last rites of a wound healed with the souls of the dead
As both our headstones read-
" Gone into the darkness and lost with the wind is a love of mine,
It melted and froze my soul,
We were a broken infinity, a lost bond, and till we meet again
Goodbye, lover. "
We stand at the cemetery gate, together for the last time in this lifetime.
The fire dies and we watch our leftover feelings go up in smokes and ashes,
Naive are the people who anticipate Graves cannot be temporary homes-
If anyone ever asks me I'll show them your letters-
Letters of everything gone and buried and unloved

9. Never Same

You stepped in like a drop of water on a barren land-
and maybe I was foolish enough to crave more,
you numbed the pain when I need it and your thoughts saved me from some self destruction-
[*I fell into them till I was safe for myself*]
turns out you worsen me too.

10. Canvases

Between polar opposites, where you disappeared
I sit this evening smoking a cigar
It's raining since the day you left
It scares me it would wash all my sins away
Tonight it rains blood, the flowers bloom
And with the roses -
Trying to consume all your touches [I know the hunger would still persist]
I call you through my bruised lips
Remember you had said once ?
" I don't like wrinkles "
Now you know not to speak the truth again
I try to paint the cosmos with our playlist.
So the stars hum carols when I'm gone-
I'll always want you a little more than I want myself-
I paint the dawn till it becomes a setting dusk-
And yet when night falls I crave your arms-
Maybe the love I have for you is too less for my he[art]

11. Isn't love a war of humanity too?

You and I- We are fallen cities,
Searching for a love that's never homesick.
Making promises that are difficult to keep.
The windchimes around my house sing notes of heartbreak,
Early morning whenever I see a text from you,
They sound like a warning.
You wander in the balcony,
At 3 in the morning.
How do I tell you that I dont have enough love to give you,
Enough hope to heal you.
I have seen people leave me cause they couldn't keep up with what I had become,
A heartless monster,
How do I tell you that Emily Brontë was right,
I'll worsen you someday,
I dont hide my tears anymore,
As I blatantly ask you if you are going to stay?
You nod your head and hold me tight,
You ask me to trust to you and I say maybe someday,
You promise to show me how forever feels,
"Ask me anything you want " you whisper,
And all can I ask you is
"Will you really stay?"

12. Palates that bleed

Lavender poison and bronze flesh,
The sky tonight has absconded its identity for the winds
Cold heart and an amethyst ring
Winter this year has realized it isn't good enough for love
So, When the sky cried and flooded oceans
Midwinter froze them, walked with dainty steps and in a small voice said-
This is not who you are
Maybe the sky wasn't pure and white when it wasn't in love with Frost.
Scarlet twisted and burned as if there was a knife stabbed in its heart
And with its fear of abandonment
It slept as the Caucasian canvas held it in its arms
Stroking her hair and putting her into a deep sleep
From afar it all looked like a bloodshed
the canvas did Dream of horrifying endings
And when it questioned about the horrors,
Scarlet said- You don't know what I was without you.
I am war and damage that you have chosen to love.

13. A lost entry

25th March, 2022

Its been a year,

Your memories are sweet and earnest, comforting like a refuge

All to a fault.

They are like the rays of sunshine

That blind you

Penetrating through the walls of this dungeon

They are like echoes on my shores [but echoes eventually fade away]

Sounds of cautious abandonment nudge me-

We wake up another day in a world, where we are strangers.

14. A lost entry-II

7th April, 2022

The archived chat still has your contact
A hollow haunted smile and nothing
This mist is a warning
You said that stars were nothing but illusions
And we lose a part of us in each of them
Tonight the Opihucus stands stills, shining brighter than ever
Asking " how could something be rarer than me ?"
The murkiness slowly cremates me in itself
As I sit looking for you through the skies.

15. A lost entry-III

25th December,2022

I am fumbling through a half love that left me under a willow tree
You were a momentary heartbreak
And I let some moments slip away....just like that
Knowing how I had run into your arms
Like a love-deprived child runs to a family that visits the orphanage
Only to see them leave at sundown
Your love killed me and maybe I chose life over love
And that's the only lie I tell myself
For questions I wasn't brave enough to ask
And choices that you never let me make

16. Love and Crosses

You smell of precious poision,
And something I would hide from truth.
You say whoever leaves first will be free-
And with that you turn into butterflies that smell of death.
Under the white blossom that sings,
We yearn to stay but truth cannot be hidden,
Tonight we are cowardly fools in love.
We hide. We walk away. We cry.
Our fears stab us , as we realise loving takes courage to stay. To fight.
Our demons set out the lights .
We are afraid of dark and things like us, we are afraid of things we love.
Knowing that they have the power to break us,
We cannot allow ourselves to fall.
Tonight this silence kills us and we chose dying over seperation.
We drift away, forever. We cry
So tell me do we really kill what we love?
Or do we kill ourselves for love?

17. Loudness silenced

Momentary silences-
You used to love me quietly in the gaps between my letters-
Telling me love doesn't have to be heard by the world-
But just by us-
You wove my smiles into a house-
Slowly picking every thread and memory-
Tonight there's an eerie silence-
I live with the thought that it's your love-
But I no longer leave gaps between my words-
For maybe when you don't find me in your heart
You'll shout out into the world to look for me-
Maybe once again Just for a night-
In the silence
you'll remember to love me

18. Orchids.

These clouds swirl and twist in vast skies,
Like cotton candies; icy interiors of your promises and
All those unfinished kisses
That lay slain In my backyard-
This rain freshens the grass around the grave of our love,
Memories grow thorns on what we once called forever-
A million galaxies bursting in your eyes,
I drink up that last touch,
It leaves a vast thirst for more-
Circling my broken ribs,
We disappear into an abyss of monsoon,
Just like the Earth swallows every tear of the sky,
And then loves it some more.
There are some golden ghost orchids,
Tonight as I sit on this Volcano watching us fall,
Wrapping themselves around me- they say to hold me is an enchant,
Evaporating into a million broken mirrors of silver hue,
I search in these brightly lit stars for you,
The cry of quiet hope, says it's already morning,
Nature becomes a heartless timekeeper-
Everyday in and out,
Everyday a little bit,
I watch us fall in love,
You watch us fall apart,
So today I ask you,

Are you sad? How was it?

19. Gift Wrapped Scars

The dusk is beginning
And I, a heartbreak -finally have the audacity to knock at your door
You let me in, a welcoming smile
You keep me in your arms, asking me how I would like to leave
You harm me, kill me, damage me
I realize I was at the wrong door
I keep going back to you
You tell me you aren't affected by things that have been broken before

20. Westerlies.

Wind breathed like life was meant to be lived alone,
It rushed as if it was having a detour.
Through the cold afternoons and crowded gaps.
It suffered to speak words – words that were so rusty, yellowed and cramped in the dark.
Almost like it was afraid to bleed ; like the words were made of glass
Yet I filled a storm in myself,
And it kept me alive, all through the night.

21. Religion.

You ask me why I am this way
sometimes I still visit that girl-
she stretches her hand- keeps drowning
she asks God if she is a monster---
hoping he'd tell her that she is good and kind
but even he doesn't seem to reach her.

22. We.

To think about you is fire and peace
And tonight I burn myself to keep US calm.
1:23AM

23. Letting Go.

The thunderstorm that I have been
I burn in my own rage
Ripping apart my home
I see you escaping me, the cities I love loathing me
" Danger, storm alert "
Through these years I have been a mere unwanted visitor
So tonight I am the fire, I am the light
And to the person who loves me
Do not come into my messy canvas
If you do not come as the blue that accepts me!
The tumultuous rain I have been
I have heard heartbreaks through glass doors that bleed the people
I have washed away the blood from their words
I take away a sinner's guilt as I fill colours in them
I turn into a grey murky cloud again
As I fill them with a rainbow
And colours that they never knew
This morning it was indigo, garnet, mauve, fuscia and hazel wood.
I have been the monsoon
And I have seen summer and spring-thc winncrs
And winter and autumn -the heartbreakers
I have seen post war cities and peaceful families,
I have seen words go to battle against feelings
And how neither of them had won
I have heard screamed silences and silent screams

A dead father's stuck son
A one sided lover's unsaid poetries
A girl who failed her parents
A rape victim that has scars too deep
Tonight I am full of these
I have been called various names
And yet when I scream,
I see no one who can understand my language
So, Who am I? What am I?
In this war of worlds and seasons
Tonight,
I am nothing but collateral damage.

24. Bougainvillea.

The trees fell as if having flashbacks of their worst fears; as if reminiscing the old wounds,
The shades of turquoise and yellow and bright green- lost in the shades of grey for so long
The pain growing inside them till at nightfall it tore them apart
They trembled and crippled in the dark,
Yet I stood right underneath the orchard
As I fell to the ground
All my noises and agonies suppressed beneath their damage
Accompanied by the relief of knowing that I couldn't fall any further.

25. Rose colored window panes.

The rain poured as if it was dismantled
Hoping it could collect all the almosts and create a story out of them,
It was certain the vestige memories were disappointing it.
Yet it kept falling – over and over and over again,
It's drops hitting the glass panes until it felt like hardwood-
Until there was nothing left.
Yet I kept drenching myself,
Searching for my story in the scraps,
Looking blankly at the emptiness the longest night beheld.

26. A Known Stranger.

Your touch- an ancient ruin that I long to see,
We- A shuffled deck of cards that I'm too afraid to read.
Tonight as you walk hand in hand with the beautiful girl next door,
I crave your impermanent stay a little more.
And These stars turn into mirrors of silver hue,
They break to grant my wish of becoming yours,
You capture them all for her-
And yet again-
The whole cosmos felt betrayed.
Holding her hand you count yourself lucky,
It's unfelicitous love,
That in this life I remain a dreamer and you and I strangers.

27. Drunk and in love.

when I am on the bar table...

And someone asks me why my glass is empty..

I shrug and say..." The wine I desire isn't made for me ".

I say I know this since long and its forgotten but undoubtedly shed a tear or two.

Not giving them a chance to ask about you...

I run out into the chilly wind that smells of you..

I try to capture a gust of it at least...

And again ... you,the wine, the magic,the nights,the laughs, your avenue...

I ain't the one for them....They aren't made for me....

There is someone else for you!!!!

28. Goodbyes.

The stillness of a winter evening
Let's say our goodbyes in the darkness
There's no need for promises
Let's walk away, to a stranger land
To a different ending!
We'll forget each other after a drink or maybe two
But surely keep pictures of our rides in gift boxes
So one fine day, down the memory lane
You'll smile seeing me and I will instantly recognize you
Remember when I told you " I dont believe in love "
And you replied "Me too "!
Let's cherish this one-day's love
The rave parties won't make us believe in forevers
Your arms won't give me the solace I find only and only in myself
We both know " walking into the sunset " it's baggage, it's too much
Let's write poetries of your exes and mine
Toss it in the deep waters, only to keep them buried in the cracks of the waves
Sit on shifting sands and caged souls
Empty hearts and empty bottles of wine
Let's be momentary soulmates
And pour out everything, let's get lost in each other
And in those pop songs, dances and the evening
Because we'll never see each other again, like a one time flight friend
Let's be story tellers

Cause tell me, how often do we bump into known strangers?
Tell me things I wish I hadn't known
I'll spill some secrets too
For before our tears dry up and smiles fade
We'll be long gone
But make sure....you don't say something to make me stay.
We both know we will eventually walk away
The last time we see each other
You tell me something that'll make me guilty
I'll tell you something to make you shudder
We walk away with what we had come
For the sea doesn't keep anything to itself
And our hearts don't welcome emotions
The stillness of a winter twilight
Half of it is you.....the other part is me
Soothing winds, in the background a singer croons " let her go "
We walk away causing darkness
In the cosmos and somewhere in each other's hearts
You walk east.....I west
We let some moments slip just like that
And back in your world and mine
Letting go is for the best!

29. She.

There was someone else for you..
Someone out there in this vast world of billions!
Writing, drawing,fading and feeling for you..
Someone inebriated.... like I was intoxicated.
The inestimable wine was you...
Alas!! The glasses were two...
They clinked each other with a frown..
The motto was the knock the other own down..
Destinies were answers...
Feelings and emotions mere illusions
You were the magic. I the wand. She the wand..
Her being universe's favourite...
Nature concluded to rupture our bond.
Yet, I still have your intoxication dancing on me.. And like you said..
I still create...
I have patience for things..
Not for you to come or something...But I wait !!
I still believe that forgotten things are not to be cried but laughed at...
But when I am on the bar table...
And someone asks me why my glass is empty..
I shrug and say..." The wine I desire isn't made for me ".
I say I know this since long and its forgotten but undoubtedly shed a tear or two.
Not giving them a chance to ask about you...
I run out into the chilly wind that smells of you..

I try to capture a gust of it at least...

And again ... you,the wine, the magic,the nights,the laughs, your avenue...

I ain't the one for them....They aren't made for me....

There is someone else for you!!!!

30. Hushed Truth.

A beer bottle at the edge of the bed
Loud thumping noises
The footsteps echo every word you said
Halluncinations bind me to this hatred
As I look at you for love
Your smile our talk of hope
Touching you is too much pain now
Suddenly the bottle bursts full of guilt
And before I know you push me down a cliff
When you held me it was pain; but getting freed is no relief either
The blur blue waters; I cry for dead memories
Maybe you let go because you loved me?!
Or maybe you were a mere memory, that I lingered too long in....
Relishing the ache
For all my words and wounds to burn slowly in the sun's wake
No, I don't wanna know the truth
For I want to love you for a few moons more
I will let you be a myth that generations will remember,
Tell me we were a mere mistake
Tell me that the forevers don't exist anymore
And I'll believe you, for I am a non believer of love too....
Love changes us they say
Construct a contrary to it
Tell them parting changes us too
Let's walk hand in hand, souls lingering someplace else

Let's be a myth that tomorrow tells
They would know what love is
Our little secret is that forevers don't exist anymore
But let me love you a few moons more!

31. The other person.

A letter to someone who had him,

I'll never know why you let him go.

When I was in the hospital last week, he brought me flowers- yellow roses.

Thorns pricked his finger, he bled a little but then kissed my forehead [whispered your name] and felt some peace.

My heart monitor beeped loud and all that love that I wanted was lost-

Some in the moment and some in the thoughts of you.

He tells me everyday, pulling me close - I don't what I'd have done without you. Keeping the locket you brought him back from Birmingham- a little more closer.

I've heard that story a million times. Of how beautiful you had looked and how he had admired you.

Pretty much like the way an orphan speaks about family. Words tumbling of out his mouth- he spends hours picking the scars you gave him.

And then wears my smile and kisses me.

He is a poet you know?

He writes in future tense, about everything he wants.

But he writes about you I know-

He writes to you every week, I know that because he was always a poet with a muse. A single muse and I was never that.

He once looked down, held my hand and whispered " I want you". I know he wasn't talking to me.

So here's a little glimpse of a life you left behind. His eyes glisten with the hope you don't know exists and I-
I hope you see him someday- Or maybe I secretly hope he sees me someday.

32. Cityscapes, Darkness and Mistakes.

City lights cry themselves to life as they realize darkness never loved them. I tell you we are the same- equal parts of love and loss.

You hold me in your eyes, when the clocks tick away and there's a dead silence in the halls- when time bends in lament- the cosmos gives up on us. To hold me so close is danger it warns you.

Human existence is nothing but a grave of misread love.

Every morning after 3AM, I become a faint shadow of everything you want, I realize it's never enough but- I turn myself into a little chrysanthemum on a winter evening,

Everything that's good in me and all that light I stole from the things I adored. I creep into your garden right outside the window of your bedroom.

I see you bleed as my words from the previous night slit your throat. I try to be good but your blood turns me into a bed of roses.

It is your nature to love me at my worst and my curse to destroy everything that makes me better.

I prick you yet again. A deathbed of a possible love story,

I become darkness again- without you there doesn't seem to be a new beginning anymore.

You become yet another city light as you wait for another chrysanthemum ,

I morph you into me, my hate lives in your heart now.

And that's how I live a little everyday.

33. Chasing Skies-looking for you.

You are letting me melt through you embrace,
Whilst keeping me in your blood shot eyes.
loving you was like capturing the running clouds-
I fear loving you now,
For I can no more kiss goodbyes with utmost maturity.
I‘m sitting on the barren and dead pages, That were devoid of moonlight
But you gave my darkness it’s permanency,
And probably it looks better;
Because what you seek is seeking you
Momentarily you stroke my hair and smile at me.I feel you beside me.
But I cant really see you-
My legs hit the rocks and you’re smiling there in those planktons.
Who have their light buried under the water,
I’m here scraping your name off the walls.
And I'm losing a little lov3 of mine
my bare hands are bruised and blooded....
An I now qualified enough to hold yours?
You are that rumor that I won’t want to die.
You say you’ll come back to receive love whenever you can-
You say, you see your naive self in me,
Walking away-
Till we meet again, For some trade of love and flicker of light,
Let’s be in dark; I’ll be regretting

And you will be in graves, burning yourself , dying everyday.
And for the time being we'll be alright

34. Firsts.

I look at you through these transparent barriers,
You smile carefreely;
Wanting to know what's in your head-
I admire you silently.
A stranger sitting at the opposite table,
You seem so lost, in a world beyond my reach.
This silence is deafening and we push back these waves of a possible love,
Afraid that they might drown us.
Our past conversations try to catch up with our present,
This vague Friday evening, passing through wilted breeze and unknown calmness,
My eyes find solace in your gaze and somehow my homesick words find their way back!
All my fears fade away, in hopes of something real,
I discover what believing feels like,
As you hold my hand and look away-

35. I ramble words as dusk sets.

Looked like you cared,

Those smiles felt like they were kept treasured in royally crafted and richly ornamented teak Boxes

The serene walks and rain drop reflections

You ripped my conclusions apart,

And my whole being alongside the question of my existence- Hanged in between you and me-

And the rope of "why "is breaking us apart

The sand in the timer is accelerating down [it reminds me of our physics classes together]

The confrontation seems and doesn't seem as an option to me, *I'm afraid my velocity won't be uniform enough to pick the pieces that would then be orphan*

And you would soon return to where you started, Probably the displacement of fragility would be zero.

Remember how you would listen to the rustling leaves and screeching crickets

Saying " this is how quietness looks "-

And I shrugged and laughed it off (how could noise be quite quiet?)

And now that you're out of sight, I know that it's your silence, That makes that atmosphere sound like nothing

Probably sometime I broke your heart-

Sometimes regretfully hating my own decisions, Calming my racing heart, With burning whiskey-

Desperate, addicted, hind sighted, non narcissist, distorted and as you used to say " you are everything I'm not "-
I still have an ounce of belief in you-
[Just like the last puff of my menthol cigar; The last sip of my 100 pipers]
Now I know why my addictions bring you back to life every other day,
And until I pass out I find myself repeating,
I'm sorry to my unknown lover,
I could never understand your f[lawless] love.

36. Happily Ever After.

There will never be a right time
I play your words on group like a sad song compelling myself to get hurt day and night by listening too much
Your memories have turned me into a mosaic of what ifs and maybes,
Now I am unsure what love really means
Does it mean basking in warmth or does it mean burning myself to keep you content ?
does it mean crossing oceans to run into your arms or drowning in a never ending Whirlpool of your scars?
I have questions and I spend in finite pains looking for answers- to compensate for my own unhappy ending
I create a contrary where your heart still belongs to me
maybe even in that universe they won't be a right time *but in a finite moment hiding from the fate that awaits us I will have my happily Ever After*

37. To,

To the one who got away...
Promising an overmorow love!!
Hey there, I know how it's going...
But as you're an English freak here I am asking!?
And because I can't be straight forward in feelings ..
Lemme start by asking about your destructive drinks...
Past is something I wake up to everyday,
I feel an urge to come, show up at your door..
But habitually I push it away!!
Remember t'was ages ago....
The breeze still brings a lump in my throat ,that I swallow...
Probably you still have those half feelings for me...
Remember you said "The world is a chaos and we're disaster's recipe....."
And these words are like liveliness...
To the wall of vacuum I have built...
For your memories to drift....
And I feel like I am trying to be a part of the word that has been constantly pushing me aside..
My ink sobs words, the cold weather freezes them on the paper...
My senses are up in smokes, they float in front of me....
Hanging like a question mark....
Quite something like our love....
That was left hanging on the wall of hopeless lives....
But till now, it does look like an art...

You turned my fucked up mess...
Into a masterpiece...
your smile made my eyes sing...
Like some beautifully crafted piano keys...
And wherever you were guilty and messed up... ..
Saying there's nothing there in you..
Your voidness touched my words and
I knew all these poems concluded with you...
They still do...
Like this letter I'm writing to you...
Maybe you would read this with a absolut nearby or...
Sitting near the grave counting each and every lie...
Years have passed down the lane...
And I hope you are lying next to somebody who knows how to love you like me....
I hope you have found the love you were to receive...
And someone you wouldn't destroy, someone who wouldn't leave....
And I sit here folding this letter..
This time I won't unsend words...
That's some of my bravery....
I explain to a muffling me...
To unpack and leave....
To a street where no one knows none...
For why stay in a place where our dear ones don't recognize us...
And yes! .... I'll make sure in a universe beyond reality we'll be 1-1....

38. Falling.

It rains

And all your dead touches, that fail to liven me up anymore- Lie untouched in my backyard,

With some promises that were slain,

I lose hope about your very return ; She is miseries that roam in you relentlessly,

you are lost in your own self

You say it matches the downpour.

There's a gift box in the attic...

I wonder if that's the kind of love you would come with,

Hundred thoughts in my head, you are ninety nine-

I fill myself a glass of wine [Did I just say return?]

I keep hallucinating, maybe

I sit on the terrace-

Wondering if these many buildings watched me fall in love?

And if they did- are their cracks and ruins a testimonial of us?

39. Meet Me Soon.

There's this petrichor and I have myself drenched in vintage feelings...
That aren't prevelant in your "feelings and emotions coinciding" world!
..
The wind slows down... As if mocking at me the words I shouted back at it...
They sting... Specially....remember the word "us"!??
(Maybe it's lying with our last take care)....
I wont call it a game.... But you played too safe and fair!!!
You have been a macabre metaphor..
Yet playing my heart in pizzicato...
The aura of broken hearts traces the nomadic leaves of this night....
And you have been like the unknown yet comforting ambience....
Like the note you sent to me....
Which covers my heart like pericardium...
Being in my soul.... Yet out of sight!!!
I sit here on the edge of my terrace....
Tryin to connect the dots
To reach your heights of extremity...
Where I'll understand if I fell myself or have I been pushed!??
This place in your heart is hardly visited...
So am I actually attracted or have I been rushed...
Do I really want you to leave....
Or have your incorrigible desicions and fears
Transformed me into a quiet Questionnaire ...
Or have I been really hushed?

Millions of phrases in my mind...
Asking for you to complete themselves
Remember how you held me in the storm,
Promising to love till the rain pours and night stays....
Well it's dawn and I feel the last drops drying up.....
And I wake up....
But here in my insides.... The rain is still pouring it's still darkness....
So... Can I ask you for a favour?
if not outside in the universe....
Pack all you have.... Everything...
I'll be all yours...
Meet me in my soul...????!

40. Warnings.

I drive through these empty streets;
Looking into the rear view mirror,
We sit on the couch at home, lost and found at the same time,
Suddenly the past looks nearer than it ever was-
For a moment we look like something more than we ever were.
I breathe in the fear as it fills into my veins,
I know if I talk my words would bleed.
There's a bad road ahead my GPS warns me, it sounds almost like you,
Showing me the dangers yet leaving me unprotected,
I raise the accelerator and grip my steering wheel,
A single tear trickles down my eyes; my knuckles turn white,
A single question in my head " Where did I go wrong, mom ?
Why do you hate me ? "
Is it because I wear my sadness so visibly, that you're ashamed?
I doubt the things you said when you were full of rage,
I resent a love that is lost forever,
For your love was always an aftermath of your anger,
Like shattering a city and bringing two bricks to build a mansion.
You ask me " If you could go back in time would you? "
Perhaps I would
Perhaps I'd do everything differently- and maybe then I'd be enough.

41. A Wanted Death.

I look at the waves,
Lying somewhere in those waters,
So many parts of me,
Scattered; broken; indecisive; crazy
They go back and forth and back and forth,
Just like my thoughts.
They circle around every sand particle and every seashell,
Hoping to find a home,
Ironic to what it is;
Tonight the sea of my past doesn't have a shore.
The lines of your palms soak up my darkness,
But I taint you in the process-
You chased my thoughts but my heart ran all alone.
The skyscrapers feel like light years,
The moon cries for me, it's guilty I'm alive;
My thoughts are tides; they eat up all your memories and each of my sins,
They invite me too;
And tonight I set the cosmos free,
I walk in.

42. Home.

Sometimes the kitchen of my house echoes with the recipes you mumbled into my ears, like a prayer for salvation -
I try not to pay attention, worried it might wash all of my sins away[*maybe I'm not ready to lose you yet*]
The echoes grow louder as the night falls, maybe our late night dances were their favorite too, the eggs in uppermost tray- crack themselves-
They hope you're hungry. [maybe that's all wanting someone feels like - destroying yourself for their hunger]
People say forevers exist-
I create a Frankenstein monster this Christmas eve, just to prove them wrong-
I fall for you once more-
[foggy milk bottles filled with tears; I think its unfair but you say that's how you like your tea]
So, I drink up my hurt in your favorite recipe of the eggnog and wish my kitchenettes some peace.

43. Ancient Maps.

I ask my dad if that's how humans exists- defying the gravity of hurt and yet wanting it more
He tells me that's how people love,
Slowly picking up the red threads of living and tying them on their wrists [wanting to be trapped in something that they love]
He says when the threads die- love becomes paranoid- searching for any parallel universe outside its lover- just to exist.
When the cemeteries smell of contempt, he says love never dies, but turns into warnings that linger,
Maybe maps and globes are nothing but unrequited stories of decades of love gone wrong, maybe they are all the paths that separated -
I think that is why the universe expands and keeps expanding, to make place for all the paths unknown,
Never healing, maybe sometimes a wound just needs to be a wound.

44. One Last Time.

This night air smells of questions, I wasnt brave enough to ask
And words are heartbroken, they didnt leave me-
I traded love for my protection,
But forever stings just as much as never does-
And for a pleasant bright morning like you
I am just a dipping sun
only having nomadic nights to give
So, look back for one last time
before the metaphorical yellow woods diverge us; Meet me at twilight's darker stage
And freezed cosmos, we could burn all the moments,
before I take you down to the greyness with me,
I will seep into roads of parched feelings.
So before it's day and night,
Before the never starts, and forever hurts,
Before you run into a mirage of past,
Lets have a lifetime, And after the day is really over,
I will walk away with my words
Believe me I'll be fine,
And even though forevers arent my thing,
I ask you to look back one last time.

Connect With The Author.

Thank you for embarking on this poetic journey with me. Your support and engagement mean the world. I'd love to connect with you and hear your thoughts on the poems, your personal reflections, or simply to share our love for the written word.

Feel free to reach out through any of these.

Email: mmohita2005@gmail.com

Social Media: dessicated_whispers

www.ingramcontent.com/pod-product-compliance
Lightning Source LLC
LaVergne TN
LVHW041238150826
845673LV00008B/2427

* 9 7 9 8 8 9 1 8 6 1 5 2 7 *